STRANGE PLANTS

Angela Royston

Heinemann LIBRARY

First published in Great Britain by Heinemann Library
Halley Court, Jordan Hill, Oxford OX2 8EJ
a division of Reed Educational and Professional Publishing Ltd.

Heinemann is a registered trademark of Reed Educational & Professional Publishing Limited.

OXFORD   MELBOURNE   AUCKLAND
JOHANNESBURG   BLANTYRE   GABORONE
IBADAN   PORTSMOUTH NH   CHICAGO

Designed by AMR Ltd.
Printed and bound in Hong Kong/China by South China Printing Co. Ltd.

03 02 01 00 99
10 9 8 7 6 5 4 3 2 1

ISBN 0 431 00202 9

British Library Cataloguing in Publication Data

Royston, Angela
  Strange plants.– (Plants)
  1. Plants – Juvenile literature
  I. Title
  581

  ISBN 0 431 00202 9

Acknowledgements
The Publishers would like to thank the following for permission to reproduce photographs:
Ardea: I Beames p14; Bruce Coleman Limited: A Compost p10, K Taylor pp20, 21; Garden and
Wildlife Matters: pp4, 5, 6, 7, 8, 12, 15, 16, 19, 22, 23, 27, J Burman p26, K Gibson p18,
J and I Palmer p11, S Shields p13; Chris Honeywell pp28, 29; Oxford Scientific Films:
D Allan/Survival p9, W Cheng p19, T Middleton p24, K Sandved p25.

Cover photograph: Gerald Cubitt, Bruce Coleman Limited

The Publishers would like to thank Dr John Feltwell of Garden Matters for his
comments in the preparation of this book.

Every effort has been made to contact copyright holders of any material reproduced in this book.
Any omissions will be rectified in subsequent printings if notice is given to the Publisher.

Any words appearing in bold, **like this**, are explained in the Glossary.

Contents

What makes plants strange?

Some strange plants look extraordinary.
Others have a strange way of living.
You will find out why these plants are
strange later in the book.

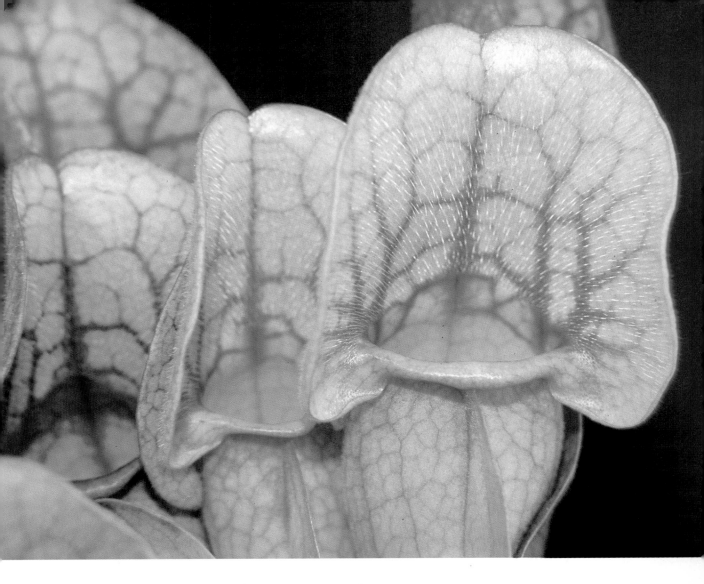

Strange plants are different from most
plants in some way. Most plants have
roots that grow under the ground,
stems, leaves and **flowers**.

Strange ways of growing

As well as underground **roots**, mangrove trees have special roots that grow from the trunk down to the ground. These roots help to prop up the trees in the swamps where they grow.

All of these banyan trees grew from one trunk! Roots grow down from the branches into the ground. They become new trunks.

Storing water

Plants need water to stay alive. Some plants which grow in dry places take in water when it rains and store it. This saguaro cactus stores water in its fat **stem**.

Baobab trees grow on dry plains
in Africa. The trunk swells with
water during the rainy season, and
shrinks again during the dry season.

Strange flowers

A Rafflesia plant has one of the biggest and worst smelling **flowers** in the world! Its foul smell attracts flies which spread its **pollen**.

The Titan Arum flowers once every six years but its huge flower is worth waiting for. It grows up to 3 metres high and then opens for only 2 days.

Stealing food

Most plants make their own food, but some steal from others. The **roots** of this dodder plant grow into the **stems** of the heather and suck its food.

Can you see the mistletoe growing in this tree? It takes some food from the tree, but it also makes food in its own green leaves.

Living together

Many plants live happily together.
Orchids grow on trees in the **rainforest**
and have long trailing **roots** that
collect water from the air.

Lichen grows on stones and trees. It is really two plants that cannot survive without each other. One of these plants, called green alga, makes food for both of them.

Living with ants

Some plants live with animals. Can you see the ants on this strange **gall**? The ants feed off the gall and stop other insects from attacking the tree.

Ants also live inside the swollen **stem** of this ant plant. The ants feed on the plant, and in exchange they spread the tree's **seeds**.

Thorns and stings

Many plants are eaten by insects and larger animals. Some plants protect themselves with thorns or stings. Just look at the prickles on this thistle!

The leaves and **stems** of this nettle are covered with tiny stinging hairs. The hairs inject poison into any animal which brushes against them.

Catching flies

Some plants eat insects! The red leaves of the Venus' fly-trap attract insects, but when one lands the leaf snaps shut.

The leaf stays closed for about 10 days, while the plant oozes a powerful liquid which **digests** the insect.

Pitcher plants

These pitcher plants are a deadly trap for insects. The inner walls are so slippery that once an insect crawls in, it can't get out.

The insect drowns in the liquid that collects at the bottom of the plant. Its body slowly breaks up and is **digested** by the plant.

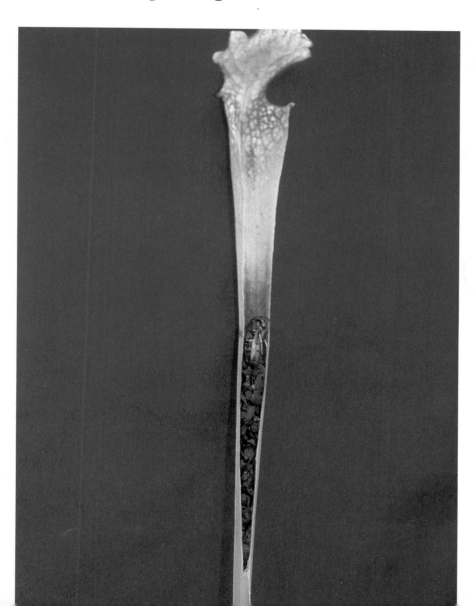

Plants that hide

Can you spot the plants hidden among the stones? These desert plants store water in their **stems**, but thirsty animals don't see them among the stones.

When it rains, the pebble plant
quickly bursts into **flower** and spreads
its **seeds** before the animals become
thirsty again.

Fantastic fungi

Mushrooms and toadstools are **fungi** and they are not really plants at all. They can't make their own food, but feed instead on living or dead things.

Most of the fungus is invisible. The
part you can see is called a fruiting
body because it produces **spores**.
Many fruiting bodies are weird shapes
and bright colours.

Growing a mould

A mould is a kind of **fungus**. You can grow a mould on bread in about a week. Leave a slice of bread on a plate all day.

In the evening pour half a cup of water over it and put it into a plastic bag. When the mould has grown, examine it through a magnifying glass.

Plant map

a strawberry plant

flower

fruit

roots

leaf

stem

an oak tree

bark

leaves

roots

trunk

Glossary

digests   breaks up food into tiny pieces so they are small enough to pass into the body of a plant or animal

flower   the part of a plant which makes new seeds

fungus   a living thing which grows from a spore and is like a plant except that it feeds off other dead or living things

gall   a growth produced by a tree around eggs laid by an insect

pollen   grains containing male cells which are needed to make new seeds

rainforest   rainy place where many trees and plants grow together

roots   parts of a plant which take in water, usually from the soil

seed   a seed contains a tiny plant before it begins to grow and a store of food

spore   the cell from which a new fern, moss or fungus begins to grow

stem   the part of a plant from which the leaves and flowers grow

Index